Reflections

of

A

World

of

Reality

the
revised edition

by
Rod L. Hollimon

Urban Thought Books
.
Atlanta

Dedication

To my Paternal Grandmother,
The Late Mrs. Aliene Hollimon Bland
No one can stop me now…

Thanks

First and foremost, I would like to thank God for giving me the talent to write and the will to share my testimony with the world. I would like to thank my family for being there for me through all of my trying times. I thank also Mrs. Crystal Harris, Kristina Roberts, and Marilyn Joyce for helping to make the first edition of this book a reality. Without the first edition, there could have been no second or third. I thank also the faculty, staff, and students of T.W. Josey High School for their continued support and for allowing me to do my very first book signing in their media center.

I thank Mrs. Diane Gilyard and Mrs. Clara Calloway for believing in me as well as my writing. I thank Mrs. Lettie Love and Ms. Crystal Lowe for their continued support and advance patronage for this edition of Reflections of a World of Reality. I thank also Mrs. Audrey Spry and everyone else who believed in me and had faith in this project. I love you all and God bless.

Table of Contents

internal tears

Grandma

Motivation

On Love

Sad Vision

Resting Place

Forward

Reflections of a World of Reality was published in its first edition (hand bound) in August of 1996 just after I graduated from T.W. Josey High School of Augusta GA. I'll be the first to admit that sharing my poetry/life with the world was not my idea. In fact, when I started writing, I didn't want anybody in the world to see my work because I wrote mainly about my life – the few good times and the seemingly overwhelming bad times. I wrote about the pain, anger, and frustration that came with being me - a good kid who happened to be in not so good circumstances. I had no idea that the words I wrote down on those little pieces of paper – sometimes in pencil or even crayon – would eventually have such a profound effect on those who read them. There were a few who encouraged me to move forward with my writing because they thought my poetry was decent; however, an overwhelming majority of the people who encouraged me to move forward did so because they could relate to the things I wrote about. They were akin to adversity, struggle, poverty, the effects of drug addiction/abuse, and even homelessness. I realized after I started sharing my work that in telling my story in poetic form, I also told their stories. With that knowledge came a divine understanding of the purpose of my writing as well as a sense responsibility. I knew that it was no longer up to me to decide if I would continue to share my work. God chose me - as ironic as it seemed at the time- to tell my story and share my poetry/life in as many formats as possible to as many people as possible. That, in a sense, is how the first edition of *Reflections of a World of Reality* was conceived.

After a very successful local run of the authentic hand bound edition of *Reflections*, it was professionally printed, and placed on the bookshelves of independently owned bookstores across Georgia. Shortly thereafter, I began speaking to youth groups, middle schools, and high schools about my life, my poetry, and how I was able to turn negative circumstances into positive realities. The more I spoke about it, the more I realized that my early poetry was really a true reflection of my world of reality. Even after I released my second collection of poems in 1999, *The Coming of Dawn,* there was still this overwhelming need to continue promoting *Reflections of a World of Reality.* There was something about it that was genuine – something between the covers that went beyond the literary realm. In fact, many of the poems in *Reflections of a World of Reality* aren't literary at all. A large majority of them are very emotional. They were written when I didn't know very much about poetic structure, meter, rhyme schemes, or any of the other things that were drilled into me during college. Once I did learn though, I discovered that there were some things that I inherently did all along that connected me to this long line of literary ancestors. I also learned that there were certain elements in my writing that could not be taught – things that no professor could accurately provide 'how to' instructions on

– things that made my poetry somehow different from most of the things we read. My poetry painted a solid picture of what I was feeling during my childhood – anger, pain, sadness, frustration, joy, determination, and happiness. It was all there – unadulterated and void of critical influence. Pure.

It is that purity that I wanted to preserve in this revised edition of *Reflections of a World of Reality*. I wanted to go back in and further exemplify those things that made the earlier edition what it was. Though I did make a few very necessary corrections, I left most of the grammar as is. I did not want this to be an entirely different book. I just wanted it to look better and be a bit more personal. I also wanted the new cover to reflect the actual tone of the book. The first cover was there because that's what I could afford at the time and it served its purpose; however, this new cover had to make a statement. It had to be poetic as well as metaphoric. I designed the cover from a painting by a very talented artist by the name of Robert Lee who just happens to be a relative of mine. He gave the painting to me as a gift for my accomplishments during a book signing in Augusta GA.

In addition to a few corrections and a new cover, this revised edition also has background information provided before select poems. These are the poems that I read most often during my motivational speaking – poems that have stories behind them or came about as a result of some tragic or emotional event. I wanted to include in the revised edition as much of my motivational presentation as possible. The student response and feedback from these presentations lets me know that there is a group of young people who need to hear what I am saying. Just as I stated earlier, in telling my story, I also tell their stories. The following letter is from a high school student in Atlanta GA:

> *Dear Rod,*
>
> *What you did for our class the other day was very inspirational. Most of us here at . . . High School are dealing with problems similar to yours. See, my father is also an alcoholic and a drug addict. He is currently not living with us now, but he is hurting my family daily by his absence. But seeing you overcome all those obstacles just gave me strength to stand up and keep on fighting. Thanks!*
>
> *Sincerely,*
>
> *A Motivated Student*

This is just one of the many reasons I am obligated to keep sharing my poetry and my life with both the young and the old. After reading the introduction, hopefully you will know my story and understand why I have to share it. After reading the poetry that follows the introduction, maybe you too will then see the poetic 'reflection of my world of reality.'

Introduction

Rodriquez Lamar Hollimon was born in Augusta, Georgia, on June 1, 1977. His mother was only fourteen at the time of his birth, while his father was seventeen. Both parents tried their best to take care of their new responsibility, but due to a lack of experience and lack of finances they could not do it alone. They decided to give his paternal grandmother, the late Mrs. Aliene Hollimon Bland, custody of him at the age of three. They felt it was the best thing they could offer him at the time. For the most part they were right. His grandmother instilled in him discipline, manners, religion, respect, ambition, and pride. She taught him how to love. Everyone in the family and in the neighborhood looked to her for strength and comfort. He lived with his grandmother until her passing in 1987. It was hard for him to cope without her there by his side offering her warm consolement and encouraging words. He spent the next year with his father, who was suffering from drug addiction. That year, Rod felt the pain of both drug addiction and the street life of Augusta Ga. Seeing what drugs did to his father, Rod made a vow to himself that he would never have anything to do with them.

His father left town about a year after his grandmother's death - leaving his responsibilities on the rest of the family. After his father left, Rod's great aunt decided to take him in.

She would provide for him a good home, great food, and plenty of company. She was the "Mama" of that side of the family so everyone lived with her. He got the chance to meet many of his second and third cousins. Being there reminded him a lot of being back home with Grandma.

After a year with his great aunt, he went to live with his uncle. This was a different environment. His uncle was single and lived alone. This was also new for his uncle because he didn't have any previous experience with children. After going through everything he experienced with his father, Rod was rather shaken up and emotionally drained. He had developed a quick temper, and a cocky attitude, while his uncle had a very low tolerance for any kind of attitude. They had many disputes -some verbal, and some physical. The Christ in his uncle, and the three hundred pound weight difference always settled the physical disputes.

After living with his uncle for about a year, Rod started thinking of his future. It was then that he began reflecting on his grandmother's teachings and how she used to tell him he could be anything in the world he wanted to be. He remembered that she always said "if you put your life, and your problems into God's hands, He will make everything alright." So he did just that. He joined organizations at school and participated in any sport he could - all the time putting God first. Rod's grades gradually went from D's & C's to A's & B's. Everything he did, he did well. People around him couldn't believe it was the same little bad, chubby, dark skinned child they had known a few years earlier. His accomplishments began to exceed his imagination.

After completing middle school with numerous athletic as well as academic accolades, Rod went on to T.W. Josey High School. There, he continued his success in the classroom and on the football field. It was at T.W. Josey where Rod began to take writing serious. He wrote about everything that happened in his life. He wrote about overcoming adversity, doubts, and just plain bad luck. He wrote about his parental situation and how it affected him. At this point in Rod's life, he began to understand what his grandmother meant when she had said, "every thing happens for a reason." He was beginning to see how the hard times that distorted his vision as a young child only prepared him for his future. Throughout Rod's four years at Josey, he received numerous academic awards such as: Who's Who Among American High School Students, All American Scholar, National Honor Roll, Georgia Certificate of Merit, and the American Achievement Academy Award. He belonged to a number of clubs and school organizations such as: the Academic Decathlon Team, Drama Club, Chorus, Peer Mediators, Student Council, the Gifted Program, and the National Honor Society. In his senior year at Josey, he served as Vice-President of the Chorus, Co-President of the Student Council, and President the National Honor Society. In sports, he received MVP of the 1992 Junior Varsity Football County Champions, All Area Football (three years in row), McDonalds Scholar Athlete of the Week, Augusta West Rotary Club's Billy Prince Award (which is given to the top athlete in the city of Augusta GA), All State 1st Team, Josey's Golden Helmet

Award, Best Running Back, and Georgia's 1995 AAA Offensive Football Player of The Year. Rod set school records for the most yards rushing in a single season (1700), the most yards rushing in a single game (267), and the most career rushing yards (3600). He helped lead the football team to the school's first ever AAA Football State championship with a perfect 15-0 record.

Rod graduated in June of 1996 with an over all GPA of 4.0,which placed him fourth in his class of 184. Just over a month after Rod graduated from Josey, he published the first edition of *Reflections of a World of Reality*. Rod Hollimon is destined for success.

internal tears

*Sometimes I laugh hard
to keep people from seeing
my internal tears*

Reality <small>age 14</small>

Reality is like a wingless bird
flying through the sky.
Just when you think the dream is real,
You open your eye.

Reality is like a thief in the night
that takes all things.
It's like a wicked witch
that steals all hopes and dreams.

Reality is like swimming in an empty pool.
Sometimes I wonder why reality seems so
cruel.

Reality is like a dream deferred -
A nightmare that came to pass.
Is our world of reality real,
Or will we wake up at last?

A Thought _{age 13}

Sometimes I wonder why things happen as they do.
Why is there so much pain and hard times to go through?

How come the world seems like a big fairytale gone bad?
Why did the problem of drugs have to fall on my dad?

Why can't we feel no ways tired
like the old church song said?

What's wrong with my people?
Why are they all falling dead?

"About Me" and "I'm Blessed" speak about my childhood and how I had come to view my situation. I began to realize during this period in my life that even though certain things happened to me, I was still one of God's children and would be okay. It was also during this time when I really started reflecting back on some of the things that my grandmother had instilled in me. I was slowly beginning to understand what she had always meant when she would say, "everything happens for a reason." Everything I went through during those years made strong enough to handle anything that would come in the future.

About Me age:14

My name is storm
Because I've been through
so much rain.
My past is unforgettable
Because I felt so much pain.
My present is unbelievable
Because no one thought I could.
My future may be limited
Because death is understood.

My talents are great,
For the Lord blessed me well.
He showed me the world
And through my pen I'm able to tell.

Love is in my heart,
But hate is on my head.
My best friend stayed by my side,
But now lies an empty bed.

So many pals by my side
Now that the path is bright,
But when the road was rough
and the pain was tough
No one was in sight.

I'm Blessed age:15

My mother left at two.
What was I to do?
The Lord held my hand and carried me
through.
Yes...I'm blessed.

My Father was addicted and left at ten.
My mind grew strong
And my heart would mend.
Yes...I'm blessed.

I was a problem child –
Not sure which way to go.
I became an athlete
And the dream began to show.
Yes...I'm blessed.

My grandmother died
And seemed to have left me all alone.
I dried my tears and remembered that I must
carry on.
Yes...I'm blessed.

My Lord has molded me for only the best
And I thank him dearly,
For Yes...I am blessed.

"Who's to Blame" was written at a time when I questioned everything. I always asked 'why me?' Why couldn't my home situation be perfect? What did I do that was so wrong to deserve my circumstances? Why was God letting this happen? Why was he not making it stop? Did my mom not want me? Was my dad on drugs because of me? Will it ever get better? Whose fault is it? Who can I blame? These were constant questions that lived in my mind. They would visit me sometimes on a nightly basis and a lot of times cause me to cry myself to sleep. The three poems that follow "Who's to Blame" are also from that period of questions.

Who's to Blame? age: 14

My life is hard… I can't explain –
For all the pain, who's to blame?

Should I blame my mom
For no being my mother?
Or should I blame society
For cursing my color?

Should I blame my dad
For getting on the wrong track –
Going away for so long
And still smoking crack?

Or should I blame my neighbor,
Who says' he's my friend –
Stabbing my in the back
Just so he could win.

Should I blame the world

For being such a place –
Promising me liberty,
But lying in my face?

Should I blame the man
Who's selling all the dope?
Or should I blame the one
Who brought it in by boat?

Should I blame God
For allowing this to take place?
Or is it the devil in his
Wicked old place?

Should I blame myself
For not going insane?
Or should I stop wondering
Who's to blame?

Just Different is a poem that really represents my personality. At a very early age, I came to the realization that I was different. It was a rather harsh realization at first because it wasn't my own discovery. Children have a rather rude way of identifying members of their peers who are not like everyone else in the group. It could one day be the only kid in the class who has glasses. It could be the one who is a bit chubbier than the rest. No matter the difference, kids will single you out, make fun of you, exclude you from their clubs, make you feel horrible – all because you're different. That kid was me for many of my childhood years. I was always the chubby one. I was always the one who didn't really have the best clothes, the best anything. It made me miserable back then. Later, I not only accepted the fact that I was different, but I praised it. I grew to love the fact that I was never like everyone else in the crowd. After a while, a few of those kids who thought I was the ugliest thing in the world, started to think I was pretty cool - all because I was different.

Just Different age: 15

I am the boy with an imaginary friend.
I do have pride,
But I hurt inside.
I'm just different.

I'm the man with nowhere to live.
I don't have money, but I have knowledge to give.
I'm just different.

I'm the so-called ugly duckling in a flock of beautiful doves.

To me I'm just fine and I have much love.
I'm just different.

I'm the outcast in society
whose family was never there.
It was unfortunate, but my God will always
care.
I'm just different.

I'm the son whose father smokes dope.
My mind is strong and I can cope.
I'm just different.

I'm every black person
Cursed from the start.
I still my color, my mind, and my God.
I am just different.

Different <small>age 15</small>

Different dreams
and different hopes
different styles for different folks

A Purpose For Me age 15

I could have died that day
when you said what you said.
You knew what you meant.
You wanted me dead.

Everything I ever hoped for fell to the ground.
You scarred my life by putting me down.

I'd rather be stoned or hit in the head!
Nothing hurts worst that what you said.

A sword is mighty…as mighty as weapons come,
But nothing is more fatal than a loaded tongue.

I could have remained down and accepted defeat.
But I was strong. God had a purpose for me.

I Wonder age 16

I wonder if the pain
Will some day go away.
What worries will remain?
Which prayer am I to pray?

I wonder who finds rest
In all these turbulent times.
Whose answer is the best?
Who hears the silent chimes?

I wonder who'll bring
Sunshine back to Earth?
What song shall we sing?
What is my life worth?

I wonder if the rains
Will come and go again –
Easing all the pain -
Starting another end.

I Wonder if the laughter
Will resume after a while.
Is this my final chapter?
Have I smiled my last smile?

"The Ocean Spoke To Me" is a poem that I wrote on the shores of Cocoa Beach Florida on our senior trip during my last year of high school. Although it had been a vacation, I was very depressed. I didn't really know why I was feeling down, but the moment I laid eyes on that beautiful body of water, I was tranquilized. I think I had been to a beach once or twice as a young child, but my previous memory of it was nothing compared to what I experienced that day. That day the ocean and I made a connection.

The Ocean Spoke to Me age 18

Yesterday I stood alone —
Alone by the wide wide sea.
I cried with tears of pain,
And bits of agony.

I cried out to the water -
Hoping to let my anger free.
That's when I heard a voice.
The ocean spoke to me.

I was astonished by the silence
That made its voice so strong.
The ocean knew my emotion.
It told me to carry on.

The ocean said a prayer
And I knew that prayer was the key.
I listened and listened closely
As the ocean spoke to me.

As I listened to the ocean,

I heard something that I knew:
The ocean and I were alike.
The ocean has pains too.

The ocean tries to speak to us all,
But only the keenest of ears will hear.
The ocean itself has emotions.
The ocean even has fear.

The ocean has a story to tell,
But only to those who can relate.
The ocean seeks consoling,
And I need a listening mate.

The ears of the ocean are open wide,
Yes wide as the big blue sea.
I'm glad I cried out to the waters,
For the ocean spoke back to me.

My Prayer is a poem that I wrote after years of contemplation about my relationship, or the lack there of, with my parents. It was sort of like a concluding prayer request to God. I wanted to stop hurting for not having my mother and father around, but I didn't want to love them any less. I wanted to live my life from that point forward knowing that my success or failure depended solely upon my decisions. If I was to fail miserably at life, then I was to blame. If I were to have enormous success at life, then I was to blame. I concluded that I didn't want it to matter that my parents weren't around for me when I felt like they needed to be. I wanted to succeed any way. I wanted to be the best at whatever I chose to do. In this poem, I asked God for it all…and he gave unto me whole heatedly all of the things I asked for.

My Prayer age 15

Oh heavenly father who are in Heaven,
I speaketh now unto thee.
Let not the life of my mother
and pain of my father speak for me.

Lord let me suffer no more
For the things they've said and done.
I'm trusting you to be there for me
And let me be second none.

Lord let me find comfort
In the life that I might live.
Teach me how to give to others
The love that they could not give.

For I am one of sound mind

And a heart that wants to love.
Please take away my pain and give me the
strength to rely on your help from above.

I wish no harm on them,
For it is their blood that I possess.
I love them just as you do God,
So my heart wishes them the best.

Lord I thank for your understanding
And always holding my hand.
Through the rain and through the pain,
You've made me a strong young man.

Life Goes On, age 15.

Yes, times are hard
And the pain is even worse,
You said "a winner never quits,"
Yet you want to quit first.

Yes, you have problems,
And so do we all.
You told us when times were hard
To stand up and walk tall.

Yes, your New Year started off wrong,
And life left you heart broken.
"Rise up and be strong."
Those are your words that were spoken.

So you feel down
And at the world you're angered and torn.
So what must you do?
Give up hope and let your family mourn?

You must hold on to your hope,
For it is now that you must be strong.
Don't let your problems get you down.
Just remember that life goes on.

I'll Cry For You <small>age 16.</small>

I feel your pain,
Your skies are blue.
Down came the rain…
I'll cry for you.

Wake up and live!
Your life must proceed.
What must I give?
What do you need?

You can't push the world away
No matter what you're going through.
Please don't mourn today.
Let me…I'll cry for you.

Your stars are bright.
Won't you let them shine.
Bring your light to the night.
Give us peace of mind.

So lift your voice and sing.
Show the world what you can do.
Don't worry about a thing.
I'll cry for you.

A Prayer <small>age 14</small>

Lord take my body and give me life.
Take my headaches and clear my strife.

Lord take my brain and fill it with knowledge.
Take my talents and send me to college.

Lord take my tongue and let me taste.
Take my soul and fill it with grace.

Lord take my pains and give me laughter.
Take my pen and write my chapters.

Lord touch my mouth and let me speak.
Open my eyes and let me seek.

That holy kingdom from which I came…
Please send me back again.

Give Thanks, age:14

Lots of shelter.
Lots of Love.
Lots of blessings
From the Lord up above.

Lots of hard work,
And lots of rewards.
For this we all should give thanks
To God our Lord.

One Day was actually one of my first poems. It was written when I was in middle school as an emergency homework assignment. I say emergency because the actual homework assignment was an essay. There were a few very good personal reasons why the essay would have been difficult to complete the night before; however, the main reason it wasn't done is that I simply forgot to do it. Realizing that I didn't have my homework assignment 15 minutes before class, I started writing this poem. When I got to class I turned it in at the bottom of the essay pile. Amazingly, the teacher accepted the poem in place of my essay. Before leaving class that day she asked if she could hold on to it. Of course I didn't have a problem with that. I was just elated that I didn't get a bad grade for not having my home work. A few months later, she held me after class to read a letter that came from the Richmond County Board of Education. It congratulated me on winning the Augusta, Richmond County, School wide poetry contest. This poem that I wrote in less than ten minutes was selected over hundreds of other poems as the best that year.

One Day age: 13

One, oh one day
Everything will be okay.

All the pain and suffering
Will soon be no more,
For one day we all shall dwell
On heaven's floor.

One day the grass will be greener,
The air will be clearer,
And all wickedness will be forced
To look in the mirror.

One day, oh one day,
We will have to answer to no man.
That will be the day when Jesus
Takes us back to the Promised Land.

Thirteen age:13

Thirteen is not just a number.
For some it is the age to remember.

All the childish and playful things are through –
Only to make room for all the new.

When you're thirteen,
Half of your childhood is all used up.
Before you know it,
You're all grown up.

Fantasy Life age:13

I love life and it is sweet.
I even love the dirt beneath my feet.

I love the stars and the silver moon.
I love the sunsets in late afternoon.

I cherish the life that God laid upon me.
I love every plant, bush, and tree.

I love the way the birds fly through the sky.
Everything is beautiful in my eye,
But for everyone else I can not speak,
For God made every life wondrous and unique.

Grateful _{age:13}

Lord you gave me life
And yes I am grateful.
You cleared my strife
And yes I'm grateful.

For Grandma...

She loved me so much
That she made me love me too
I owe her the world

Loving Memory _{age 14}

You gave me shelter
and showed me your love.
You showed me your grace
Of God up above.

You dried my eyes when I cried.
You tucked me in bed.
You gave me a kiss
And a Band-Aid when I bled.

You, that great person I love so dear.
You made me feel warm when you came near.

For you are the one,
who still loves me more than anyone can.
God bless your soul
Mrs. Aliene Hollimon Bland.

Grandma's Message is a poem that I wrote around the age of 14. The poem is actually a recount of a dream that I had shortly after my paternal Grandmother died. In the dream, I remembered being very afraid, but my grandmother comforted me and assured me that everything would be alright. After the dream, I remember waking up with an enormous amount of courage. I felt as if I had just been given a mission – a mission that I was adequately trained for and knew I would be victorious. That dream – along with the image of my grandmother comforting me with her warm arms – shall be with me until my mission is complete.

Grandma's Message <small>age 14</small>

My dear son, I speak to you from above.
In your heart I feel much love.

Don't gather hatred for the ones who strike hard.
Just give them love. It's okay, for you'll play it smart.

Stand tall and hold your head up high.
I know that you'll succeed...all you have to do is try.

And even if you fall face flat in the dirt,
Stand up quick! Don't let them see you hurt.

For you are hope and the future is in your hands.
Don't hold yourself to being just a man.

Don't just be a man. Be much more!
Dig deep inside and hold your feet firm to the floor.

Straighten your shoulders and lift your chin.

Look to the Lord and then begin:

Don't say a word,
Just remember what I say.
Strive to be the best
And you'll make it in the world today.

You'll Never Die age 17

You'll never die, no matter what they say.
I know you're here with me today.

I feel your presence in all I do.
The things you taught me, I see them through.

I hear your voice every time the wind blows.
You'll never die, and our God knows.

You're with me when my nights are cold and wet.
I feel your warmth and your comfort I'll never forget.

I see your smile when I look up in the sky.
You're in my heart...you'll never die –

Not even when I'm torn and my body is old.
You'll still live deep down in my soul.

I felt your pain when you said goodbye.
As long as I live...you'll never die.

Dedicated to my Paternal Grandmother, the Late
Mrs. Aliene Hollimon Bland

Father Be Strong is a poem I wrote and dedicated to my father J. L. Hollimon, who began suffered from the deadly disease known as drug addiction at the age of 14. While it is true that his illness caused me and the rest of my family a great deal of pain and heartache, I know that I am who I am because of it. His drug addiction is, in a sense, what saves my life over and over again. If I had not dealt with life under those circumstances when I was a child, it would certainly tear me from limb to limb right now. I also gained a lot of wisdom from those experiences. If I didn't know anything else in the world when I was a child, I knew I didn't want to be "like my daddy." After seeing what drugs did to him and all of us who loved him, I didn't want anything to do with them. Some say that experience is always the best teacher. No one ever said that the experience had to be your own experience. I learned about life mostly through my father's negative experiences. I sometimes view him as sort of a sacrificial lamb. If his only purpose in life was to show me which path not to choose, then his living, his suffering, his addiction was not vain. "Father Be Strong" is my tribute to him, for God has truly blessed me through his suffering.

Father Be Strong age 17

I for give you for the pain.
I forgive you for the sorrow.
I thank you for my last name.
Your day will be better tomorrow.

Don't give up hope.
Your laughter will come soon.
I know you're able to cope.
God will mend your bitter wounds.

I know your days are long,
And your nights seem to never end.
Just hold on and be strong.
You'll break that deadly trend.

Father I say be strong.
I know your intentions are good.
You will be able to live as you like
And choose your own neighborhood.

As long as you keep the faith
God's word will prevail.
He's going to show you a whole new world,
And all that's good will unveil.

Everything happens for a reason.
God knew you'd survive the test.
God showed me the world through you.
Now I know which life is the best.

The lord works in mysterious ways,
But the job is always well done.
I would not be as strong as I am
Had I not been your only son.

So I thank you father once again -
Again I say be strong.
The Lord is on your side forever.
He'll take you all the way home.

to J.L. Hollimon, my father, who taught me a lesson I could
never have learned in a classroom - a hands on lesson about
life, struggle, failure, and success.

Achieve, Until We've Won, Spread our Wings and *I Can* are all poems that I wrote for myself as well as for my high school football team. We were about to attempt what the entire city thought impossible. We were attempting to turn an inner city football team with a history of embarrassing records into a state powerhouse. The year before I wrote this poem, the football team's record was 1-9 (1 win 9 losses) so a large part of the city's negative attitude toward the possibility of the team actually winning was somewhat justified. The purpose of this poem, however, was to uplift the team's attitude. I knew that before anyone else would believe we could win, we had to really believe in ourselves and know beyond a shadow of a doubt that we could and would win. When that season was over we were 4-6. It wasn't exactly a winning record, but we won the respect of all of the teams we faced that year. Many of the games we lost we lost only by a few points. The following year, we were the region champions and went on to the state playoffs. No one believed, but we did indeed...Achieve.

Achieve age 16

I remember one day someone said
"You won't do it as long as there is a sky."
I thought to myself: what are they saying?
I'll do it as long as I try.

They said it couldn't be done
Because it's never been done before.
I had no doubt that I could
And I would do much more.

Sometimes I wonder why people just don't

believe.
Still I laugh because I will achieve.

And when I do they'll come running
Like they were with me when I began.
I won't brag or boast and tease or toast
Because I am a better man.

I'll just look them in their faces
And turn away with ease.
They didn't believe,
But I will indeed achieve.

Until We've Won _{age 17}

My fellow eagle athletes today I applaud
A year of success brought forth by God.

Hard work and dedication –
Yes, those were the keys.
We overcame all odds
And celebrated many victories.

Many people wanted, hoped,
But still disbelieved.
We kept the faith in our hearts
And all of our goals were achieved.

Now today, as we look back on
what we've done,

Lets be proud,
But not content,
For our journey has just begun.

We must set higher goals,
And strive to reach bigger dreams.
We must be strong and never give up,
No matter what the future brings.

At some point it may be hard,
And nothing will be fun,
But when the road is tough and our bodies
are tired,
Lets not stop until we've won.

Spread our wings age 16

My fellow teammates I congratulate you thus far.
Lets be the eagle of prey and reach for the highest star.

I know no one else believes or even cares what we do,
But we must believe in ourselves all the way through.

Even when we're down and the road seems far far away.
We need to stay strong and stick together for we are well on
our way.

We must keep our hope and let our pride carry us through.
Our dreams are before us, but we must make them come
true.

We all know that first is first and last is last
So lets be second to none and last to laugh.

We must spread our wings and soar to new heights.
Lets beat all the odds and by God win the fight.

Much like the previous poem, *I Can* was written during my high school football career. It was inspired not only by all the negative things people said about my football team when we were re-building our program, but also by all the negative things people said about me during my childhood. "I Can" was the answer to all the negativity that I encountered. As a child, I was always told what I couldn't or wouldn't be able to do. I was told I couldn't be successful in life because I was poor and I lived in the projects. I was told I couldn't make it out or through the ghetto without selling or using drugs because I was a product of that type of environment. I was told I probably wouldn't make it to college because I wasn't smart enough or I wouldn't live that long. I was told I couldn't be a running back in football because I was too slow. The negativity that I faced as an individual was mirrored by the negativity that the football team faced. We were told that our team wouldn't be successful because we were "a bunch of inner-city thugs who didn't know anything about winning." We were told that we wouldn't win because it "wasn't realistic" for us. Even after we made it to the state playoffs my junior season, the negativity continued. One Augusta GA news anchor went as far as to laugh out loud on live television during a pre-season interview with one of my teammates who said we would be 15-0 at the end of the season. After a rather long chuckle, the reporter replied "Son do you really think that's a realistic goal." On the night of December 16, 1995 that same reporter said on live TV, "I can't believe it. The 1995 T.W. Josey Eagles have made history tonight - capping off a perfect 15-0 season with a victory over Cedar Shoals. The T.W. Josey Eagles are Georgia's 1995 AAA State Champions." This one is my personal favorite.

I Can _{age 17}

They say my task is impossible.
There's far too much doubt in this land.
Nothing to me is impossible
As long as I believe...I can.

I've been through trials and tribulations.
Adversity knows where I lay.
I've known disappointments and frustration.
I've overcome obstacles in my way.

Often I enjoyed the doubts,
For they made me a better man.
I know that I'll never be without.
As long as I believe...I can.

Hard times are often before me,
But even they won't make me stop.
I'm determined to reach my destiny.
I'll make my way to the top.

They said my dreams wouldn't come true,
But I always stuck to my plan.
There's nothing on earth that I can't do.
As long as I believe...I can.

To Reach the Clouds _{age 18}

Where do we go from here
Now that the game is won?
What bright future lies near?
What great life just begun?

We must set new goals now
And work harder than before.
We must take on higher roles
And find different roads to explore.

We will maintain our height
For Eagle pride is in our souls.
This won't be our final fight,
For there's much more to unfold.

So keep your wings steady
Even if you don't seem to fly high.
Know that you're the best of the best
Make sure that your limit is the sky.

There will be life after Josey
And we all shall soar above the crowd.
There is no mountain we can not climb
If our goal is to reach the clouds.

Rising Class is a poem I wrote and dedicated to T.W. Josey High School's Class of 1996. We were always underestimated, but we never underachieved. For every negative story the local newspapers chose to print about us, there were twenty success stories that will probably never make the headlines. Since I graduated from Josey, I've been in more than a few cites - seen and met more than a few people – some "educated" – some "successful" and some who are even wealthy; but the people I went to school with at Josey are still some of the most intelligent people I know.

Rising Class age 17

Oh rising class be proud and stand tall,
For you're the best class of them all.

I see hope in the eyes of all of you.
I smell success in all that you do.

You are the future – the hero in every child's dreams.
Through you, the world will hear freedom ring.

Rise high and be strong.
Keep moving – even when the road seems long.

Just look to the Lord and let your limit be the sky.
Be proud of what you are, A senior at Josey High.

You <small>age 17</small>

Don't let yourself down.
You've put too much in YOU.
Don't take away you're crown,
For you're work is not through.

Now is the time.
YOU have to be strong.
It's all in your mind.
YOU must journey on.

YOU must turn it up,
And work harder than before.
Winners don't give up
when there are more wins to explore.

YOU can rise higher,
And soar to a new height.
Re-ignite your fire
And let God be your light.

Dig deep inside,
And pull out the real YOU –
The YOU with all the pride-
The YOU that sees it through.

I Thought I had it Bad is a poem that actually came from a real situation. I was at a car wash in Augusta GA when a young barefooted child, who could not have been much older than 11 or 12, came up to me and asked for some change. His response after I gave what I had really made me reevaluate my own situation and the things I sometimes complain about. My life at the time was no walk in park; however, it wasn't necessarily a walk in the jungle either. After that encounter, I began to sincerely thank God for the things I did have instead of wasting time and energy complaining about what I didn't.

I Thought I Had it Bad age 17

I thought I had it bad
When rice and gravy was all that I had -
Until I saw that child with no shoes.
He asked if I had a dollar that he could use.
I gave him two for that was all I had.
He said "Thank you" kindly and put it in his bag.
He Gave a gracious smile and said "God Bless You.
This will buy some food for me and for my brother too."

I saw then that I was blessed. No matter what I had, someone always had less.

I thought I had it bad
When we had neither lights nor heat -
Until I saw that slim old man with his pillow on the street.
The only light he had was the sun that lights the sky.
He had no roof, no sing, and no warm bed in which to lie.
He owned a pillow and a sheet that he always kept close.

The little things I take for granted are the things that he'd like most.

I thought I had it bad when I looked back on my life -
Until I saw that child with more mischief and more strife.
His mother died the same day she gave birth.
Every since then, he's carried the curse.
He saw his father die in pain -
Beaten to a pulp and shot in the brain.
That made him an orphan so sometimes he had to choose
From being beaten up or sexually abused.

My problems are petty to that child whose life is hell.
I'm glad I can count my blessings and through my pen I'm
able to tell.
No matter how bad things seem to be I'm blessed,
For there is always someone who has it worse than me.

Rest At Last age 17

Let him order your steps in his word.
He will guide you and make you free as a bird.

Let him be your light, for it is his gift.
He made you sweet as rose, but stern and swift.

God gave you the ability to lead and the power to
teach,
The heart to be a mother and the spirit to preach.

Indeed be grateful and let his will come to pass,
For you are his gift to us and we shall rest at last.

How Blessed They Are age 17

How blessed they are to have your voice
There to encourage them and help them rejoice.

They are truly blessed to have your hands
There to chastise them so their future will stand.

How blessed they are to have your arms
There to mold them and hold them through all alarm.

How blessed they are to have your prayers,
For your prayers will carry them through all affairs.

It will carry them through thick and thin
And through the race of life that is so hard to win.

You give the guidance of the bright North Star.
You're a strong black mother.
God knows how blessed they are.

Great Wise One is a poem that I wrote as encouragement to a person who had often encouraged me. In writing this poem, I realized how much of a burden it must be to be the person who is responsible for encouraging others. What things can we say to lift up the people who always lift us up in times of need? In some cases, it is our parents or guardians. Sometimes it is our teachers, religious leaders, family, or even closest friends. But who is left to inspire the inspirers. This poem is one I wrote in an attempt to inspire one who had always inspired me.

Great Wise One age 16

Oh great wise one, keep your head up high.
Be the leader you are and let your spirit fly.

Hold on to the Lord, for He is your strength.
Keep your faith and he'll go the length.

Practice what you preach
And what you teach will be the truth.
Continue to love sinners,
Wicked ones and bad youth.

Don't let the bad days take your best.
just hold on and be strong. He'll do the rest.

So just hang in there,
even when times are hard.
Keep on praying oh wise one
And remember that your strength
is your God.

Mell's Song <small>age 14</small>

I once knew a man whose name was Mell.
Mell was caught inside a living hell.

Mell knew right and Mell knew wrong,
Yet Mell still sang a very sad song.

It was a song of mercy and a plea for help.
Mell couldn't sing aloud so on the inside he wept.

Mell kept singing,
But no one seemed to hear.
Mell was in a dual between fate and his inner-fear.

There was only one way to defeat fate and himself:
He would have give up his fame and his wealth.

To do that Mell would rather die.
Behind closed doors, in his mansion he would cry.

Eventually Mell lost the fight.
He loaded his gun and slowly turned off the light.

Todd's Story age 15

I once knew a boy whose name was Todd.
He had only two friends: his Grandmother
and God.

God, of course, would be there forever,
But he and his Grandmother wouldn't always
be together.

His parents, on the other hand
Had other issues and other plans.

Todd got older and finally realized his creed.
Despite the issues of his mother and habits
of his father, he could still succeed.

That gave Todd a motive and God showed
him which way to go.
He began to think wiser and his dream
started to show.

Todd is now a strong young man.
His mother and father will always have his
helping hand.

But most of all, he'll keep his trust in God.
And always keep his loving grandmother
close to his heart.

Smokey age 15

His name is Smokey and now he's dead.
All because crack got in his head.

Smokey swore he was smart.
He raced with danger and gave death a head start.

On a one way street, he figured he could still win.
I guess he didn't know that street was a dead end.

Smokey ran that race and sure enough he lost.
Before Smokey even entered, he knew the cost.

He knew the rate of danger and the speed of death –
The sound of thunder and the fear it left.

But that didn't stop Smokey.
See he had to get his high.
I wonder if he knew then
That he was saying his last goodbye.

On Love

To love is to stand
On the edge of laughter while
Fighting back the tears

Love <small>age 16</small>

Love is wonderful.
It is the cure for all pain.
When all else is gone,
It is love that will remain.

Love is special.
Love is unique.
Love will make a bum
Feel like a sheik.

Love is like a friend
Who will always be there.
Love will take a cold heart
and fill it with care.

Love is radiant
And warm like the sunshine.
Love is the key
To God's great design.

Experience age 16

"How do I love you?
Let me count the ways."
How long have I loved you?
Let me count the days.

When I first met you,
My mind was in a mess.
But your love has certainly
changed me for the best.

Then came that day –
The day you hit me with the news.
You said it was all over,
And I sang…sang the blues.

If I could do it all again though,
I wouldn't change a thing.
Not even the moment
When you gave back my ring.

I couldn't understand it though.
Why was this the end?
Later it hurt to find
That you were with my best friend.

It hurt me deeply at first,
But I recovered from that fall.
I guess it really "is better to have loved and lost
Than never to have loved at all."

What I feel age 17

When there is love
and I know the feeling is real,
Still there is doubt.
You say I don't feel what I feel.

When there is hope,
And I give all I can.
There is still doubt about where I stand.

My love is strong
And I know it has room to grow.
What love really means?
I guess now I don't know.

I do know what's in my heart
And I know that it is real.
Why must you doubt
That I feel what I feel?

Oh Sweet Sunshine age 17

Oh sweet sunshine
On the outside to pure and beautiful brown,
But when I look in your eyes
To my surprise I see an ugly frown.

It's such a shame that when I speak to you
Your reply is oh so very cold.
If only you knew how love could really be,
You would give it back in sevenfold.

Oh sweet sunshine I mean no harm
When I seem to stare.
I just can't control my eyes
When I know in my heart that I care.

Oh Sweet Sunshine, your beauty is radiant
Like the rays of the golden sun.
If only you had a heart,
You'd see that I too can be fun.

My dear sunshine
I know you break my heart in pleasure,
As life goes on my pains won't last,
But the memory of you I'll treasure.

Sweet Destiny _{age 16}

Was it destiny that caused our eyes to meet?
I felt helpless and you looked so very sweet.

I wanted to say a million things,
But the words just didn't come through.
I hate myself even more right now,
For I didn't say a word to you.

I saw your legs, your hips,
And then your beautiful brown face.
I think my heart skipped a beat.
I was amazed by your grace.

I did get one last chance
To ask you for name.
I opened my mouth, took a deep breath,
And still couldn't say a thing.

You left me with a feeling that I
Never had before –
A memory of a girl
That I indeed adore.

If God will grant a wish,
And it is meant to be.
I'll step into my future
And find you there with me.

Secret Friend _{age 17}

Secret Friend, you look very nice today.
You probably know that, but I'm telling you anyway.

Secret Friend, you're kind of special to me.
I know its not right, but that's the way it seems to be.

Secret Friend, I know I'm wrong for this,
but I can't help but wonder what warmth lies in your kiss.

Secret friend, this can be fun for both of us.
But we should be strong and not succumb to lust.

Maybe there will come a time when all this secrecy will end.
But I guess until that time, you'll just be my secret friend.

Lost in Her Eyes is a poem that I wrote after meeting this beautiful young woman while I was at work in the Augusta Mall. I was working at the Great American Cookie company (yes I was occasionally called the cookie man). When she came up to place her order I was almost speechless. I tried to think of a million clever things to say, but they all came out as gibberish. It was a very awkward situation and I couldn't resist writing about it.

Lost In Her Eyes age 16

I was lost in her eyes,
So innocent and crystal clear –
As bright as the sun, as wide as the sky,
Her eyes they showed no fear.

I wondered where she'd been,
For I'd never seen her before.
I could not have her as a friend,
For I would pray for much more.

We tried to exchange a phrase:
She said "Mindy is my name."
My mind was in a daze,
For I said "mine is the same."

"No, I mean it's Rod I say.
Do accept my apology.
Your smile is the best I've seen today
And no greater can there be."

"It's quite alright Mr. Rod," she said.
"I'm touched by your compliment."
She said "Good day" and I nodded my head

And said "she's Heaven sent."

Yes, her smile was so splendid I had to
applaud –
Unique as the silver moon.
My worries were gone and my stress had
ended.
I hope I'll see her soon.

My Lady _{age 16}

You, my lady are so precious and unique.
The fragrance of your perfume...so powerful, yet so sweet.

Yes you are my lady and I will honor you 'till time grows old.
This love I grant is of my body, my mind, and my soul.

My lady what I feel is oh so very true.
You see my lady I dedicate my whole heart to you.

Love Was Meant To Be _{age 16}

The moment was rare
And you looked beautiful just standing there.
First just a few quick glances…then our eyes met.
I knew right then that it was your heart that I would get.

I saw you as you saw me.
Before you, my heart was locked shut
And somehow you found the key.

I know this is special and fun
For both you and me so let's be strong
And let nothing part us in the future to be.

I hold in my heart a place where you can always dwell.
You know that I love you know and always will.

I Give To You age 17

I give to you something precious and dear
In hope that you'll ease my pains and cast away my fear.

I give to you a part of me that you can strengthen or kill.
It is at your mercy. You hold what I can always feel.

I give to you my hopes and dreams.
In prayer, we both can take them to the extreme.

I give to you myself
So that we will never part.
In your hands you hold my health,
For I've given you my heart.

Precious Blessing:
a Love Prayer _{age 18}

Lord bless her fragile and precious soul.
Let me love her and bless us until our time grows old.

Lord let this love not be in vain.
Keep our hearts strong and as sure as Heaven's reign.

Lord keep us faithful and obedient to your voice.
Let this be your will as well as our choice.

Lord be our sole provider and punish us when we're wrong.
Be with us and guide our holy love song.

Lord ride with us when our road is rough
and our character seems unknown.
Be our light and show us the right way home.

Lord let me say thank you for loving us without end.
Please let it last forever, and right now I'll say…
Amen

Eternity _{age 18}

When I close my eyes to sleep I dream.
I see you and things are as they seem.

My hope and my sunshine —these things are in you.
If we were apart I wouldn't know what to do.

When I'm down and all tired out,
Your love lifts my spirit and again I can shout.

When I'm with you all joy prevails.
Anything that tries to get me down fails.

You are my love and only you can put a smile on my
face.
I thank the lord daily for blessing me with your grace.

I can hold you for eternity and never let you go.
You are my inspiration, and I'll tell the whole world so.

My darling dearest, I'm glad that you're with me.
Know that when I say I love you, it is for eternity.

Loyalty? age 15

Why did it have to end this way?
Why couldn't it have lasted longer?
If only you had been faithful,
our love would have grown stronger.

I knew this would happen,
so I didn't get too attached.
I've been hurt too many times,
My heart couldn't stand another scratch.

You thought you were playing a smart game,
but you failed to understand
that the game can only be played on the young,
it will never fool a real man.

Sooner or later the tables will turn.
And sure enough a broken heart will be well
earned.

For then you will see
how a broken heart really works.
You see, deep down inside, it really hurts.

Memory age 15

We thought it would last forever.
we thought it would never die.
I wish it had lasted forever,
but now it's time to say goodbye.

No, I'm not leaving town,
yet I am still far away.
I wish our feelings were still mutual,
like they were on yesterday.

But my love for you now
is like the love of a brother.
I wish it was you that I really loved,
But I'm sorry...it's another.

I'm sorry it had to end like this.
I'm sorry you were misled.
I hope you find a real love.
I hope our friendship isn't dead.

Sad Vision

When I sleep I dream.
I see my race gone astray.
Sometimes I might cry.

A Walk to the Past was written shortly after I entered high school. It was written when I came to the realization that I didn't know nearly enough about the history of my people. I was taught about some of the more popular African American's like Martin Luther King, and Harriet Tubman, but there was this whole world of people that I knew absolutely nothing about. I began to realize that even though my historical ignorance was surely no coincidence, it was up to me to learn what I was not taught.

A Walk to the Past age 16

As we step into the future,
We must look back on the past.
We must remember those who made us free
at last.

I could start with Harriet Tubman,
Rosa Parks, or Dr. King.
They all touched our hearts
and gave us a reason to sing.

We know the stories of "Roots"
And we felt the cries of pain.
Our people went through so much
And still there is little gain.

When times were hard
And the pain was more severe,
Harriet kept on moving,
For she knew that freedom was near.

When the road was rough,

And the sun was more than hot,
Rosa was brave,
For she didn't give up her spot.

When society was corrupt
And most certainly unfair,
Martin looked to the Lord,
For he knew that God would be there.

Yes, we know a few of these stories,
But we do not know them all.
We need to learn out past
Or our future will be very small.

Open Your Eyes and See A and B are a bit radical; however, they are addressing not only racism and injustice, but also other major issues facing the African American community such as black on black crime and fatherless families. They both address the fact that we can not afford to act as if the problems don't exist. We must open our eyes and not only see them, but do what we can to help fix them.

Open Your Eyes and See (a)

age 17

Open your eyes and see.
This was never the land of the free.

They gave us liberty and justice to sing,
But I have yet to hear true freedom ring.

We sing the songs of glory,
But when will we learn the real story?

We all learned the same lie,
And never once asked why.

Still we wonder who's to blame?
Look in the mirror, but don't call any names.

I guess that's not us we kill.
And that's not our child whose father isn't real.

Why do we insist on remaining blind?
Why not read a book,
And cultivate your mind.

I'll try to help by starting with me,
But it will take us all to finally see.

Open Your Eyes and See (b)

age 17

Just open your eyes
to this world of deceit
Look at all the blood on the streets.

Whose blood is it?
We pretend we don't know.
Our own descriptions fit,
Yet we say it's not so.

It is ours I say.
We must open our eyes and see
What happens every day –
We against us...I against me.

It is a shame I cry!
What future can there be?
Before you die a lie
Please open your eyes and see.

Just Like a Brother addresses another form of black on black crime. I did know many people who were direct victims of violent crimes; however, an overwhelming majority of the people from my neighborhood are victims of a more tragic black on black crime. They don't necessarily die quick deaths at the hands of a person with a gun in their hands. They eventually die slow at the hands of a person with some deadly drug in their hands. These deaths are, in a sense, worse than violent deaths because the entire communities witness the gradual deterioration of people who may have been intelligent, wealthy, or even educated. A drug addict dies over and over again – as do little parts of those who love him/her.

Just Like a Brother age 17

Just like a brother
You stole behind my back.
Just like a brother,
You sold my neighbor your crack.
Just like a brother,
You gave it to your friend.
Just like a brother,
You shot him in the end?
Just like a brother,
You gave it to your dad.
Just like a brother,
Trying to go for bad.
Just like a brother,
With stupidity in his head.
Just like a brother,

Tomorrow you'll be dead.

Resting Place

Death
Life's end
Sleeping, Crying, dying
Leaving all body behind
Resting

"The Rainiest Day" is a poem that I wrote after the death of Ms. Suzan Varner. She was my high school geometry teacher. She passed away during my junior year at T.W. Josey. She was loved by all who knew her and is greatly missed.

The Rainiest Day age 17

Tragedy is in the air.
There's a feeling of bitter peace.
The students are now aware
That a great loved one is deceased.

A minister of knowledge,
For she passed on all she knew –
The sweetest teacher one could have
With energy all year through.

She was to most of us a teacher,
But to all of us a friend.
Yes, she's gone away,
But her teachings will never end.

Be happy for she's now with God
Dwelling on Heaven's floor.
Where the sun shines day and night
And nothing is a bore.

There is no need for tears,
For she would not want it that way.
Just remember her with a smile
Even on the rainiest day.

In memory of the late Ms. Susan Varner

Resting <small>age 17</small>

Will I be able to live in peace?
Will my soul ever find rest?
Will I know what's best?

Cry No More is a poem that I wrote in high school after the death of one of my classmates Shana Anthony. I actually had a small crush on her in elementary school, but I was much too shy and intimidated to let her know back then. I didn't see her much after those Lamar Elementary days until she transferred to Josey High School. We didn't talk much then, but it was good seeing her around again. She was a very lovable person who had many friends. The entire school was saddened and in disbelief when they announced that she was no longer with us due to a health condition. "Cry No More" is a tribute to those who knew and loved her.

Cry No More age 17

Cry no more loved ones and weep no more friends.
If you keep her in your hearts, her life will never end.

Weep no more, for she is in God's place.
She would not want you to cry so wipe the tears from your
face.

Cry no more when you think of her beautiful smile.
Just cherish her memory, for she made her life worthwhile.

Weep no more, for she is not alone.
She is with God and her soul sings on.
Cry no more. Just remember her while she rests.
Carry her spirit in all that you do, for she has passed her test.

So cry no more children for this is not the time to moan.
Rejoice and be happy, for Shana has gone home.

In Memory of Shana Nicole Anthony

Beginning of My End age 17

When I am done living my many prosperous years,
Please don't shed any woeful tears.

Please don't think any harmful thoughts,
For death comes unexpected - without any faults.

My parting shouldn't be one of sadness and hollow space.
It should give reason for an open heart and a smiling face.

If you don't feel I deserve roses while I breath,
please don't bother to give them when I leave.

For when I'm gone, I can take no earthly things.
I will be in a place where all souls sing.

It will be a place where mortal suffering ends.
In this place, everyone is indeed a friend.

Only then will it be time for me to rejoice.
My soul seeks eternally, that heavenly voice.

When I get there, and I will get there my friend,
That will be without a doubt, the beginning of my end.

Through the Years <small>age 18</small>

I wonder who will be concerned
When my day is sad and blue.
Who will write a poem for me
When my sad song seems to be true?

Often I am afraid that no one will even care.
When depression crowds my emotions…
I'm alone,
For no one seems to be there.

I cry out for help in ways that seem to be known.
I guess my cry is silent,
For the only cheer I get is my own.

My closest friend seems to be away,
Although I try to keep her close.
I don't know if she knows my emotions.
Sometimes I feel like a ghost.

Sometimes I cry in solitude
Until I run out of tears.
That's when I grab the pen and let it flow…
Writing has carried me through the years.

Reflections age 18

Now that I sit and look back on the pain,
What if everything had stayed the same?

I wonder which excuse would I have used.
What deadly drug might I have abused?

Which corner would have put me on top?
Which gun would the cops have made me drop?

I wonder what elder would I have cursed.
Whose grave would I dig first?

Maybe the grave would have been my own.
I'm glad God blessed me with a good home.

I'm glad I chose to live my life
Not in mischief and not in strife,

But to live in joy and have it in peace
In hope that my future will be happy at least.

And when all my days are done at last,
I hope to rest on the greenest grass.

I hope to sleep in a wonderful place
With no discomfort and eloquent grace.

And when I'm gone, I want people on earth
To remember me for what I was worth –

That I had lived my life to the fullest extent,
And that I did nothing without God's consent.

This will make me happy in rest,
So I plan to live my life at its best.

This is only the beginning

www.rodhollimon.com

Notes

<u>Notes</u>

Notes

My Favorite Rod Hollimon Poems

<u>My Favorite Rod Hollimon Quotes</u>

Other Books by Rod Hollimon:

The Coming of Dawn: a Collection of Poetic Thoughts('99, '02)

images of me ('03)

We want to know what you think about this book. To send your praise and/or critism, please write or email to the following:

Urban Thought Books, Inc.
Reader Comments
7632 Ward Lane,
Jonesboro GA 30236

readercomments@urbanthoughtbooks.com